Ray Atkeson

Ray Atkeson
WESTERN IMAGES

Graphic Arts Center Publishing Company, Portland, Oregon

International Standard Book Number 1-55868-011-X
Library of Congress Number 89-83841
All rights reserved.
No part of this book can be reproduced by any means
without written permission of the publisher.
© MCMLXXXIX by Graphic Arts Center Publishing Company
P.O. Box 10306 • Portland, Oregon 97210 • 503/226-2402
Editor-in-Chief • Douglas A. Pfeiffer
Associate Editor • Jean Andrews
Designer • Robert Reynolds
Typographer • Harrison Typesetting, Inc.
Color Separations • Spectrum West
Printer • Dynagraphics, Inc.
Bindery • Lincoln & Allen
Printed in the United States of America

ACKNOWLEDGEMENTS

I wish to express my appreciation to all my family, friends, and associates who have contributed so much to my life and photographic career. Without their help, it is unlikely this portfolio would have been published.

Especially deserving of appreciative recognition are the members of my family, whose understanding and tolerance of my idiosyncracies and my work have been so very important to me. My first wife, Mira, loved the outdoor life and the wonders of nature as much or even more than I. Our daughter, Eleanor, patiently endured long trips and the interruption of her social life for many years. My second wife, Doris, and her son, Rick Schafer, have devoted years to assisting me.

I would also like to thank Craig Carver, Larry Geddis, Scott Krueter, Larry Ulrich, and other friends who have given me invaluable companionship and assistance.

I am truly grateful to all those who have in so many ways contributed to my life and my work.

Front Cover Photograph: The Needles at Cannon Beach, Oregon, take a dramatic stand at day's end in November, 1985. A coastal landmark, The Needles have withstood time and tides.

The Top of Oregon, Mt. Hood, Oregon, 1933

RAY ATKESON AT GOVERNMENT CAMP, 1930

PREFACE

Photography is said to be the most popular hobby in the world. It has been my hobby, profession, and obsession for over sixty years of excitement, adventure, pleasure, frustrations, hardships, and thrills. It was a photo of Portland and Mt. Hood in my grade-school geography book in Illinois that first interested me in the West, and it was the magnificent, scenic grandeur of the West that made me want to take pictures.

When I was seventeen, I told my mother that I wanted to work in the harvest. She called my bluff, told me to go, and gave me her blessing. After several years following the crops, I landed a temporary job running errands for Claude Palmer's Photo Art Studio in Portland in 1928. It was a miracle for me that this turned into more than fifteen years of work, carrying me through the Great Depression and teaching me how to use a camera.

At that time, I was paid thirteen dollars a week for sixty to seventy hours of work. In the time that remained, I pursued my obsession: hiking, exploring, and photographing the Northwest. As often as possible, Saturday night found me with my wife, Mira, and friends on the road or trail. By daylight, we were often enjoying the splendor of sunrise from a vantage point in the mountains, or watching first light on the Pacific surf from a nearby bluff on the coast.

My obsession for recording on film the experiences and pleasures of the trail grew as I hiked and climbed. In the late twenties, I joined the Mazama Mountaineering and Outdoor Club. Soon after, I joined the Oregon Camera Club. Sometime around 1930, following a hike to the summit of Larch Mountain from Multnomah Falls, five of us formed the nucleus of a group we called the Columbia Hikers, later known as Wy'east Climbers. Today, much of the beauty of the Northwest is familiar to millions of people, but at that time comparatively few people had seen what I saw. I wanted to share it, and I began to send prints to editors. I sent the first prints to the editor of the *Kansas City Star,* and to my delight he reproduced my small prints of Mt. Hood in his rotogravure section and sent me a check. This was a good start, and in the meantime, I was learning the importance of quality from Claude.

My first chance to take a commercial photo came by accident. In 1931, there was an extremely cold spell and the Columbia River froze over. Marc Conway was trying to get a picture of a Crown Paper Mill boat when he fell through the ice with the 8x10 camera and the heavy

tripod. While he thawed out, I went out and took the photo, and soon after, I found myself almost constantly behind the 8x10, photographing every subject imaginable under all kinds of conditions. Once, I spent the entire morning recording damage in a ship whose engine boilers had exploded and then, still covered in bilge and with no time to change, rushed off to cover a reigning queen of the silent screen at a local department store.

The 8x10 view cameras we used in the early thirties have not changed as much as other photo equipment and film. We used a monochrome film that was known as Par Speed, but what Par was no one seemed to know. We had no meters and no understanding of ASA. The film was color-blind—it responded best to blue and white and seemed to be allergic to red and yellow. Artificial lighting for interior photos was achieved either by flash powder or arc lights. Neither was very efficient, but they did put out a lot of light. Flash powder was spread out in a flat, shallow pan and ignited by an inefficient Fourth-of-July cap and trigger, which sometimes caused extremely hazardous conditions. In the early thirties, large flashbulbs filled with magnesium foil arrived on the scene. They fired by electrical connection, and additional bulbs could even be fired by induction, if accidentally set off by friction. I created quite a stir in a department store elevator one day when an overcoat pocket filled with half a dozen flashbulbs ignited by friction and caused a sudden, intense heat.

During Franklin D. Roosevelt's first presidential campaign, Claude and I were assigned to photograph the candidate in Portland. Twilight was setting in, and Claude was operating the 8x10 view camera while I was holding the flashbulb reflector against Governor Roosevelt's face and igniting matches so Claude could achieve a sharp focus on the ground glass. With patience wearing thin all around, I watched Claude's hand squeeze the rubber bulb to open the shutter, which signaled me to fire the flashbulb. The bulb didn't fire, and Claude yelled "SHOOT! SHOOT!" You can imagine what might have happened under such circumstances today. We didn't get the picture, but we did get one after the future president's speech, with reliable flash powder.

In 1933, Mira and I took off in our dilapidated Model A Ford to visit relatives in the Midwest. We borrowed three hundred dollars from a loan shark, hoping that along with the loan our small savings would be sufficient. We had exactly thirty-five cents when we returned home after four thousand miles of travel over mostly dirt and gravel roads.

It was a great trip and included our first visit to Yellowstone National Park, the Black Hills, South Dakota, and many other western areas of interest. The highlights of the adventure were visiting my mother and brother and family and meeting editors in Milwaukee and Chicago who had published my photos. I also saw my photo, "Glacier Serac," on exhibition in the International Salon of Photography at the Chicago World's Fair. This was the first of my photos to be honored by a prestigious salon.

In 1937, a revolution occurred in photography. Eastman Kodak released Kodachrome film. Previously, color was limited to Autochrome, Finley Color, one-shot blunderbuss color cameras, and the manipulation of color filters with black-and-white film. Kodachrome opened up a new way of life, and I immediately purchased a little Bantam Special camera that took 40mm film. That same year, Mira and I and our three-year-old daughter, Eleanor, took off on an extensive trip through the Southwest. As usual, I took many shots, but only a few of the exposures I made are still in my files. The Kodachrome experienced a tremendous color shift and the film faded. Within a year Kodak corrected this characteristic, and all Kodachrome dyes since then have proved very stable. I have many outstanding Kodachrome transparencies from 1938 to the present day.

In 1941, I became preoccupied with pressing concerns. The Second World War had begun, Photo Art Studio had been classified a defense industry, and I spent a large portion of my time photographing the activities of the three huge Kaiser shipyards. It was not until after the war that I decided to pursue a career as a free-lance photographer.

Everyone except Mira and me doubted that it could be done, but my timing could not have been more perfect. The publication field was experiencing tremendous growth, and I managed to make a good living, traveling to the East Coast once a year to sell my photos for publication and spending as much time as possible outdoors with my cameras the rest of the year. Memorable associations developed with Walter Freze of Hastings House Publishers of New York, who featured my photos in a series of calendars and regional books, and with Eastman Kodak Company, which included my prints and transparencies in promotional programs and used three of my photographs for 12 x 60-foot Coloramas in Grand Central Station. Other people supportive of my career in the early days were Ed Hannigan, editor of *U.S. Camera Magazine,* and Frank Fenner, editor of *Popular Photography Magazine.*

I had lots of good luck, but good luck is not always the main ingredient in getting a picture. A lot of planning and sleepless hours studying weather charts also go into it. I've often said that we make our

own luck, and I do think we have considerable control over our good or bad fortune. The main ingredient that goes into photography is lots of hard work. A love of that work to the point of obsession is certainly a big advantage. So is persistence. Finally, there is the way a photographer chooses to approach a subject, and his technique.

Some photographers like to cover as much territory as they can, photographing as many different subjects as possible. Personally, I prefer to locate a potentially photogenic subject and concentrate on it and move around less. I find it's often possible to get two or three pictures of any given subject with a little creative study of angles and lighting conditions. The low angle of sunlight in the early morning and late afternoon creates the most interesting effect on most subjects. The main thing is to recognize the potential of the subject and study it thoroughly, deciding what light will best reveal the full beauty of the subject. This means that the photographer should be an early riser so he can be on the scene before sunrise, and he should plan to stay until the last light leaves the sky.

I shoot only positive-type film, that is, the color-slide type of film that presents the image as you see it. Negative-type film is almost impossible for the inexperienced person to visualize, but it is best for the photographer who wishes to make prints because it results in superior quality prints of certain types. Individual needs should dictate what kind of film is used, but one thing I do recommend is that a photographer familiarize himself with one variety of film and know just what it will do. This is true of camera equipment as well.

I enthusiastically recommend a 35mm camera with a couple of supplementary lenses, although I have always used a larger format 4x5 camera. This has worked best for me because publishers have appreciated the visual impact of the 4x5, but today most publishers prefer to work with 35mm. The big advantage of the 35mm camera is portability. Often, by the time I get my 4x5 set up, the situation that attracted my attention no longer exists or it isn't as good. The 35mm also has the most readily available accessories or lenses.

Today, I am using a 4x5 Linhof and a Hasselblad 2 1/4, each with four supplementary lenses. I usually use a tripod. It's essential with a large-format camera like the Linhof, and when you use a 35mm it can help create higher-quality pictures under certain conditions, particularly when you need longer shutter speed to obtain depth of focus. I also use a Leica with three supplementary lenses, including an 80 to 200mm zoom lens, a macro lens for close-up photography of flowers and intimate details, and a 28mm lens.

There are a lot of good films available—Kodak, Fuji, Agfa—but the slower-speed films, both in color and black-and-white, usually give the finest quality. We now know how well these films hold up. Unfortunately, the Ektachrome 4x5 film I used in the forties and fifties had unstable dyes, and thousands of my transparencies deteriorated. However, I also recorded some landscapes on 35mm Kodachrome, and these transparencies are still in excellent condition. But the loss of the Ektachromes was a tragedy for me, and the most drastic signal that the art of photography is an evanescent one. At the time, I had no idea my prints were self-destructing.

Every photographer is influenced by the photographs he sees, both in technique and style, and I think that we all have been influenced to a considerable extent by other photographers. I recall that in the late twenties and early thirties I was greatly impressed by the work of Leonard Missone, a world-renowned European photographer, and I endeavored to emulate his style to some extent. Ansel Adams undoubtedly influenced more landscape photographers than anyone else. He once told me that he wanted his disciples to be creative on their own instead of emulating his work, but any instructor is bound to be imitated by his students. David Muench is another photographer who has been very influential in the field.

I believe that my photography has been influenced considerably by other photographers whose work I have admired, especially those who were pursuing similar careers to mine, such as Joseph Muench and Bob and Ira Spring.

It's my belief that if you are going to emulate the work of someone else, you had better not do it too often. If you do, you should do it with a purpose. Try to improve on what you are emulating. There is always room for improvement. I have seen very few, if any, photographs in my life that could not be improved upon in some way or other. I have certainly never made a photograph that could not be improved upon. In the late forties, when Mira became interested in taking pictures and we joined the Forest Grove Camera Club, we all learned a great deal from the critiques we gave each other. During the ensuing years, that club became one of the top two or three in the country.

I guess I have always had more than a normal interest in nature. It was probably inborn. My dad spent a considerable part of his life exploring the West in search of gold and eventually settled down on a 320-acre farm in rugged land overlooking the confluence of the Illinois and Mississippi rivers. (Our farm is now incorporated in Pierre Marquette State Park.) Dad never lost his wanderlust, and I remember

him exploring the creeks and canyons and timber on our farm. When I migrated to the West, all the wonders of nature stirred the emotions of this Midwest flatlander, and that wonder has never let go of me.

Mira and I traveled to other parts of the world as well—to Hawaii, to New England, through the South, to Switzerland, Norway, and New Zealand. (Mira's work eventually resulted in a memorial book of her own.) Photography always gave us many opportunities to enrich our lives. Whether it's a profession or a hobby, photography exposes you to the world and educates you to travel, geography, geology, botany, zoology, even to industry and politics. The thing I most appreciate is the increased power of observation I feel and the opportunity I have to more fully enjoy our environment. Photography has also given me an unexcelled opportunity to affect our environment through the medium of my photos.

Following a trip through California in the midseventies, Mira became seriously ill and had to undergo surgery. I lost her a year later. During her illness and for a year or so afterward, the business of photography was the least of my concerns. In fact, I had no intention of pursuing my career any further. In 1975, Doris Schafer, who had worked with Mira and me for so long, lost her husband, Dick. Our mutual understanding brought us together, and in September 1977, we were married and started a new life togehter. By that time, I had resumed my interest in photography and, with the help and understanding of Doris, I began to rebuild. Now, with the assistance of Doris's son, Rick Schafer, and encouragement from many other people, we are on the road again. Our cameras are in action. We have made numerous fruitful trips to the Oregon Coast, to Mt. Rainier and Mt. Shuksan, to Yellowstone and the Tetons, to Mt. Jefferson and the Central Cascades, to Alaska and Utah. I never tire of revising my work on such places and I never resist my temptation to expose more film. I always want to take the picture a little differently and, hopefully, a little better every time.

But believe me, this is not a one-man show. It has taken a lot of cooperation and understanding from my family and friends along the way. There is never enough time to take care of requests or meet deadlines. There are hours, days, and weeks of travel by foot or otherwise, additional hours of waiting for the elusive condition I always hope to capture on film. My family and friends will emphatically confirm that my number one priority is my profession and hobby. And I can confirm that I could not have done it without them.

RAY ATKESON

RAY ATKESON ON MT. HOOD, 1933

Winter Sculpture, Washington, 1946

TIMBERLINE LODGE, OREGON, C. 1945

COLUMBIA ICE FIELDS, BRITISH COLUMBIA, 1941

DEER, BRITISH COLUMBIA, 1947

SHORELINE PINE TREE, OREGON, 1937

CELILO INDIANS FISHING, OREGON, C. 1955

SHEEP SANCTUARY, OREGON, 1937

One summer day, I was returning along the scenic Columbia River Highway to Portland after a day of commercial photography in a Hood River apple-packing plant, when I noticed a band of sheep grazing in pastureland near the river some distance away. Sunday found Mira and me on location searching for an approach to the sheep. Our search was successful, and we soon had my cameras in action — a 4x5 Graflex and a newly acquired Bantam Special. The latter was loaded with an eight-exposure roll of Kodachrome, which Eastman Kodak had just released to the public.

The location was the present site of Rooster Rock State Park. The sheep were cooperative up to a point, and I caught pictures of them going and coming while Mira did her best to persuade them to be more helpful. Finally, when we were exhausted, I captured this black-and-white shot as the sheep sought the shady sanctuary of an old tree. I had not yet started to think in color, but I soon would.

EYES OF THE FLEET, PORTLAND, OREGON, C. 1935

Bristlecone Pine Panorama, California/Nevada, c. 1965

GLACIER SERAC, MT. HOOD, OREGON, 1932

CHALLENGING ASCENT, MT. HOOD, OREGON, c. 1932

Fog-veiled Coast, Washington, c. 1955

13

SWANS AND CYGNETS, PORTLAND, OREGON, 1930

Only one other time have I seen Mt. Hood and Lost Lake as beautiful as they were on this mid-December day. That other day was my first visit to the lake in 1926, and then I overexposed my pictures beyond recovery.

Now I was back, after a chilling drive in foot-deep snow. The lake is normally inaccessible this late in the year, and I took the last mile on skis after leaving my car parked in the deep snow.

I feared it might be impossible to get the car turned around on the forest road when I headed back home, but my first view of the lake and mountain destroyed my concerns about possible transportation problems. My camera wouldn't quit until the last rosy glow of sunset had faded from the mountain.

MT. HOOD, OREGON, C. 1972

MT. BAKER, WASHINGTON, 1946

ROSE, PORTLAND, OREGON, c. 1975

BANDON, OREGON, C. 1982

CAPE KIWANDA SURF, OREGON, c. 1978

COAST SUNSET, OREGON, c. 1982

ECOLA PARK SUNRISE, OREGON, 1988

FISHING THE GALLATIN RIVER, MONTANA, 1947

PARADISE ICE CAVES, MT. RAINIER NATIONAL PARK, WASHINGTON, C. 1972

BARN, EASTERN OREGON, c. 1953

WILDFLOWERS IN THE CASCADES, WASHINGTON, c. 1972

Early on the morning of May 18, 1980, I heard the radio announcement that Mt. St. Helens had really blown its top and I immediately grabbed my camera. It was at that moment that fellow photographer and mountaineer Russ Lamb phoned me, and in a few minutes we joined the parade of motorists heading toward the towering inferno we could dimly see thirty-five miles to the north.

Yale Lake was our goal, but we were halted by the highway patrol just north of the town of Amboy. With the binoculars, I always carry, I spotted a logging road traversing a nearby mountainside, and Russ urged his car up it as fast as he could. All too soon we were forced to stop, and along with several others continued on foot to an open vantage point.

It was an astounding sight that greeted us. Less than ten air miles away was the eruption—clouds of ash, smoke, and gas churning sixty thousand feet into the otherwise blue sky. We watched spellbound in the mid-morning warm sunshine.

This was the climactic event of my photographic career, one that continues to revive memories of past experiences around the beautiful mountain. The devastation and now the recovery of plant growth have been the focal point of my camera since 1980 brought an end to one era and the beginning of another.

MT. ST. HELENS, WASHINGTON, 1980

NA PALI COAST, HAWAII, c. 1962

WAIKIKI SURFING, HAWAII, 1952

Na Pali Coast, Hawaii, c. 1965

FROSTY MORNING, LOCHSA CANYON, IDAHO, c. 1955

LAKE POWELL, UTAH, C. 1965

MT. MORAN, WYOMING, 1984

TETON NATIONAL FOREST, WYOMING, C. 1975

Devil's Tower National Monument, Wyoming, c. 1948

"BONSAI" PINE, ZION NATIONAL PARK, UTAH, 1987

CARLSBAD CAVERNS, NEW MEXICO, c. 1958

One late September, my friend, Jack Janacek, and I hiked in to Image Lake via Lake Chelan by way of Lymon Lake in Cloudy Pass. This was my first visit to the Glacier Peak Wilderness, and it was a long hike. We were both carrying heavy packs. In addition to camping paraphernalia, we carried a second tent for photographic purposes. I was also carrying a 4x5 camera, a heavy metal tripod, many film holders, two extra lenses, a Hasselblad camera with three extra lenses, an extra film magazine, plus a plentiful supply of extra film, flashbulbs, and flash reflectors to supplement the weak light put out by the campfires. Jack had a heavy metal tripod and a Hasselblad camera.

Our first photo was this one, taken in early evening light. That night we camped under the stars and the next morning we were up long before sunrise. Camping is no longer permitted beside the lake, due to the fragile conditions of soil and vegetation.

IMAGE LAKE AT TWILIGHT, GLACIER PEAK WILDERNESS, WASHINGTON, c. 1965

Mt. Rainier, Washington, c. 1975

NORTHHEAD LIGHTHOUSE, WASHINGTON, 1988

MT. ST. HELENS, WASHINGTON, 1982

MT. SHUKSAN, WASHINGTON, 1985

MT. ADAMS AND GLENWOOD VALLEY, WASHINGTON, C. 1975

ONEONTA GORGE, OREGON, C. 1962

REDWOOD NATIONAL PARK, CALIFORNIA, c. 1965

SUGARCANE TASSELS, HAWAII, 1972

Stream in the Cascades, Washington, c. 1975

NATURE'S CONTRASTS, WASHINGTON, 1985

A lot of planning and watching of weather maps helped to create some of my lucky winter visits to Crater Lake, Oregon. On this trip, the situation could not have been much better, although I was perilously balanced on a snow cornice extending over the lake rim. As I could not use a tripod, I made an exposure of 1/100 of a second with a hand-held Speed Graphic and comparatively slow-speed film.

CRATER LAKE IN WINTER, OREGON, C. 1965

Painted Hills, Oregon, 1979

WHEAT HARVEST, EASTERN WASHINGTON, C. 1962

CRATER LAKE NATIONAL PARK, OREGON, 1980

ALPENGLOW, MT. HOOD, OREGON, c. 1948

RAINBOW TRAIL, UTAH, 1947

MONUMENT VALLEY, ARIZONA/UTAH, c. 1945

PLEASANT VALLEY, COLORADO, c. 1971

Yellowstone Canyon, Wyoming, 1983

56

SKIING AT SQUAW VALLEY, CALIFORNIA, c. 1958

Tonquin Valley and Rockies, Canada, 1941

DELICATE ARCH, UTAH, 1987

DELICATE ARCH, UTAH, 1987

CANADIAN ROCKIES, BRITISH COLUMBIA, 1950

Autumn, Montana, c. 1965

KAANAPALI BEACH, HAWAII, 1977

POPPIES, CALIFORNIA, C. 1972

PROXY FALLS, OREGON, C. 1975

MT. HOOD AND WILDFLOWERS, OREGON, c. 1962

WATERFALL, WASHINGTON, 1986

MT. JEFFERSON, OREGON, C. 1946

Morning Mists, Washington, c. 1983

Forest Trail, Columbia River Gorge, Oregon, c. 1965

I arrived during an October snowstorm at the little hostel near timberline in Garibaldi Provincial Park. The trip from Portland to Vancouver, British Columbia, had included a boat trip on Howe Sound to Squamish, a truck ride for several miles up a steep mountain road, and a six-mile hike in a blizzard. Eventually, the weather cleared for a photograph of the picturesque hemlock trees banded together on a knoll with autumn-tinted huckelberries surrounding them.

Timberline in Garibaldi Provincial Park, British Columbia, c. 1947

ESCALANTE RIVER, UTAH, c. 1963

SOLAR PHENOMENON, OREGON, c. 1955

TULIP FIELD, OREGON, 1988

WILDFLOWERS, SOUTHERN WASHINGTON, C. 1984

Electrical Storm, Portland, Oregon, c. 1973

PACIFIC SURF, OREGON, c. 1977

OREGON DUNES NATIONAL RECREATION AREA, OREGON, c. 1975

OLYMPIC RAIN FOREST, WASHINGTON, c. 1972

CAPE LOOKOUT TRAIL, OREGON, c. 1982

SWORD FERN AND MOSS, WASHINGTON, C. 1975

BANDON, OREGON, c. 1977

SHORE ACRES, OREGON, C. 1975

Ecola State Park has been a happy hunting ground for my camera. One day as I was hiking up the trail from Crescent Beach, the clouds playing above the seashore reached a climactic display of beauty and I hurriedly adjusted a polaroid filter on my camera lens and composed this picture of weather-sculptured trees.

Coastal Symphony: Trees and Clouds, Oregon, c. 1985

Grand Canyon, Arizona, c. 1955

BRYCE CANYON NATIONAL PARK, UTAH, 1987

Monument to the Past, Monterey Peninsula, California, c. 1948

MONTEREY PENINSULA, CALIFORNIA, C. 1948

CANNON BEACH, OREGON, 1988

SUNSET GOLD, OREGON, C. 1985

SHORE ACRES, OREGON, C. 1978

OWENS VALLEY, CALIFORNIA, 1965

TULE LAKE NATIONAL WILDLIFE REFUGE, CALIFORNIA, c. 1964

Mt. Hood and Wildflowers, Oregon, c. 1982

OLD FAITHFUL GEYSER, YELLOWSTONE NATIONAL PARK, WYOMING, c. 1983

JOSHUA TREE NATIONAL MONUMENT, CALIFORNIA, 1982

It's unlikely that anyone who has visited Image Lake in Glacier Peak Wilderness will disagree with my opinion that this is one of the most beautiful mountain areas in the world. The many miles of mountain-trail hiking necessary to reach the lake are spectacularly beautiful, and the lake is a photographer's Valhalla.

The major problem is carrying enough film and photo equipment. That was especially true on my first trip, when this picture was taken at sunset on a late September day in 1965.

Glacier Peak Wilderness, Washington, c. 1965

Autumn Mosaic, Washington, 1985

CHECKERBOARD MESA, UTAH, c. 1974

LEHMAN CAVES, NEVADA, 1947

WINTER IN THE CASCADES, OREGON, c. 1948

ASPEN TREES, WASHINGTON, c. 1954

Lassen Volcano, California, 1946

GOLDEN GATE INTERNATIONAL EXPOSITION, CALIFORNIA, 1939

SEATTLE CENTER, WASHINGTON, C. 1975

MT. RAINIER NATIONAL PARK, WASHINGTON, C. 1973

DEER, OLYMPIC NATIONAL PARK, WASHINGTON, C. 1965

ELKHORN RANGE, OREGON, 1976

North Cascades from Sauk Mountain, Washington, 1977

Internationally known racer and instructor Yves Latreille skied off the crest of Squaw Peak for the benefit of my camera on a clear, February day. This was before Squaw Valley became world-renowned as the home of the 1960 Winter Olympics. It was also before scientific snow control was in effect. In later years, those snow cornices hanging above Yves would have been blasted away before skiers were permitted on this very steep slope.

Skiing in Squaw Valley, California, c. 1957

Redwood National Park, California, c. 1965

KODACHROME BASIN STATE PARK, UTAH, c. 1963

PLEASANT VALLEY, COLORADO, c. 1962

THE BLUE BOAT, MT. BAKER NATIONAL FOREST, WASHINGTON, c. 1972

SAWTOOTH WILDERNESS, IDAHO, C. 1978

Monterey Cypress at Sunset, California, c. 1965

GRAYS RIVER BRIDGE, WASHINGTON, C. 1968

NORTH CASCADES, WASHINGTON, 1986

COASTAL FOG, OREGON, c. 1964

CRESCENT BEACH, OREGON, c. 1983

The Needles at Sunset, Oregon, 1985

EAGLE CREEK PUNCH BOWL, OREGON, c. 1965

MT. SHUKSAN AND PICTURE LAKE, WASHINGTON, C. 1985

Oak Creek Canyon in Winter, Arizona, c. 1955

BRYCE CANYON IN WINTER, UTAH, c. 1955

BRISTLECONE PINE GHOST TREE, CALIFORNIA, c. 1962

ARCHES NATIONAL PARK, UTAH, 1987

CAPE KIWANDA, OREGON, C. 1965

LIDELL CABIN, MT. HOOD, OREGON, c. 1955

Snow Scene, Oregon, 1978

RAINBOW BRIDGE NATIONAL MONUMENT, UTAH, c. 1985

GRAND CANYON, ARIZONA, c. 1958

MT. ST. HELENS, WASHINGTON, 1947

Vine Maple Leaf, Oregon, c. 1965

FOREST, WASHINGTON, c. 1965

135

MT. SHASTA, CALIFORNIA, 1988

Autumn, Washington, c. 1965

137

Multnomah Falls, Oregon, c. 1982

NORTHERN COAST, OREGON, 1987

NOTES TO THE PLATES

1 It wasn't an easy climb that January day in 1933, when my wife, Mira, Ralph Calkins, Ole Lein, and I reached the crest of Mt. Hood. The day before, in a snowstorm, we had climbed on skis the three and a half miles from Government Camp to the old Camp Blossom shelter at timberline. Now the two-week-long blizzard had finally relented, and we took off early on the 13th, hoping to climb to the summit shortly after midnight without our skis.

Taking turns at breaking trail, we did not reach the crest until after sunrise, but we were rewarded with fantastic conditions. The old fire lookout cabin was encased in ice, but despite the frigid temperature, I put my 9x12cm camera into action.

2 It took two weeks of ceaseless effort by that old master artist Boreas to sculpture this and countless other artistic forms among the timberline trees on Kulshan Ridge in Mt. Baker National Forest. I captured this 4x5 with my Speed Graphic in 1946. The brilliant winter sun shining directly behind the ice-encased tree provided backlighting at its best.

3 Sometime in the forties, storms held Oregon's Cascade Mountains under siege with unrelenting fury for more than a week. Several times I drove up to Timberline, hoping the weather would break and permit me to take pictures of winter beauty with a bit of sunlight, but I had no luck.

Finally, in desperation, I made one more try. This time I went at night and took along a bunch of large flashbulbs and a flash gun, and I had no sooner unloaded the car when a full moon suddenly began to illuminate the fairyland of snow-draped trees, and the clouds began to melt away. I set up the tripod and camera, opened the shutter, and hurriedly skied to a point outside the composition where I fired a flashbulb to illuminate the snow-covered trees and my skier friend, Nap Rogue.

4 In the summer of 1941, I accompanied Walt Dyke and two other mountaineers on a trip through the Columbia Ice Fields. The climax of our adventure was to be an ascent of Mt. Columbia, second highest peak in the Canadian Rockies. After establishing our second base camp on the ice fields above the Athabasca Glacier, we set out for a ski ascent of Snow Dome. An easy ski jaunt to its 11,400-foot summit provided this photo of Mt. Columbia and the towering peaks of the Rockies.

Our decision to go immediately to Snow Dome proved fortunate. A severe blizzard attacked us upon our descent to camp, confining us to our tents for several days, and treacherous snow conditions canceled our Mt. Columbia ascent.

5 In October 1947, I hiked in to Diamond Lakes Hostel in the heart of Garibaldi Provincial Park, British Columbia, while on assignment for *National Geographic*. An early-season blizzard accompanied me on the trail in, but the weather relented and the snow disappeared in a couple of days.

This young buck apparently knew that autumn in the timberline region wasn't over and he hung around the two beautiful lakes and obligingly modeled for several pictures. In fact, he grew so attached to me that it became difficult to catch a scene without his presence in the composition.

6 In autumn of 1937, Mira and I and our two-year-old daughter, Eleanor, spent a few days at Cannon Beach, Oregon. It was a fantastic outing, and each day that early-morning beach fog I have grown so fond of veiled the shoreline. It was then, I think, that I really learned to appreciate the photographic possibilities of various atmospheric phenomena.

I captured this and other impressions on both 120-roll film and 4x5 cut film. The Carl Zeiss Company had just given me a 120 Ikonta folding camera, and I was also using my old, dependable, and extremely bulky 4x5 Graflex.

7 For several years during the thirties, the arrival of the Pacific Fleet was celebrated second only to Portland's Rose Festival. Each night during the fleet's visit, searchlights roved the sky above the harbor for half an hour and, for the benefit of photographers, the lights were kept stationary for ten minutes. Working with a camera on tripod, I went into action, catching reflections on the river and the ships themselves, such as this photo of the USS *Houston*.

8 Please see copy on page facing Plate 8.

9 An opportunity that is gone forever is graphically captured in this photo, taken in the fifties, of an Indian landing a big Chinook salmon at the legendary Celilo fishing grounds on the Columbia River. Fishing as portrayed here was drowned beneath the waters of the huge lake created by The Dalles power dam.

10 The wind-swept crest of the White Mountains on the California/Nevada border is the unlikely realm of the oldest living things on earth. Here, ancient bristlecone pines have flourished for thousands of years.

I photographed this venerable old snag above Owens Valley in eastern California during a visit made one November in the sixties. The bleak, panoramic setting encompasses the White Mountains and the distant snow-crested Sierra Nevada.

11 In 1932, Al Monner, Don Burkhart, and I were exploring the ice falls of Eliot Glacier on Mt. Hood when we discovered this spectacular serac reflecting the morning sunlight from its scalloped side. It was a natural for photographs, and we each took a turn atop the pinnacle. This photo was featured in the 1933 International Salon of Photography at the Chicago World's Fair.

12 My friend, Jim Harlow, approaches the Chute, a thousand feet below the summit of Mt. Hood, during a late-winter climb in the early thirties. It was a beautiful day in March, and we had enjoyed ideal climbing conditions en route from our overnight stay in the old Camp Blossom cabin at timberline. Several rotogravure editors around the nation chose to publish this photo as a full-page spread.

13 One autumn morning in the fifties, I took advantage of the low tide and fog-veiled sunlight to photograph a beach on the Quinault Indian Reservation near Point Grenville, Washington. I liked the compositional effects I could get with black-and-white.

14 My constant search for new and different subjects of interest paid off one day in 1930 when I discovered these cygnets in Portland, Oregon. As the rising sun illuminated the setting with cloud-diffused light, the swans proudly displayed their offspring for my new 4x5 Graflex. At the time, I was using portrait-pan film without benefit of meter.

15 Please see copy on page facing Plate 15.

16 My career in full-time free-lancing was off to a glorious start in 1946, when, after several phone calls to the Mt. Baker National Forest Headquarters in Bellingham to check weather conditions, I found myself on the scene. After weeks of heavy winter weather, brilliant sunshine revealed a gleaming wonderland, and a new acquaintance, Hugh Riley, and I took off on skies from Heather Meadows. The deep, new snow made for arduous climbing to Kulshan Ridge, miles above our starting point, but sunrise greeted us as we reached the ridge.

Our goal was the crest of nearby Table Mountain. Again deep snow thwarted our attack, so we took off to surround the mountain, hoping to find a less difficult route to its crest. Surround it we did, and in midafternoon, after miles traversing the slopes around its base, we finally made a short but steep approach. We advanced below an ominously overhanging snow cornice by removing our skis and using them as makeshift shovels to dig a tunnel. This was dangerous work, but we emerged on the vast, undulating snowfields above, where I rigged a makeshift tripod with my skis and poles and put my 4x5 Speed Graphic and 35mm Leica into action.

Our descent was a hair-raiser. We took the steep, northeast slope, which normally I would never have attempted in daylight, and fifteen hours after our predawn take-off we finally reached shelter and rest.

17 Portland's International Rose Test Gardens are a paradise for botanists, photographers, and those who love floral and landscape beauty, and I have spent many enjoyable hours there with my Hasselblad. For close-up shots, I prefer to work with my 150mm lens and supplementary lenses, which make it possible to fill the film area or, in this instance (a photo taken in the seventies), to include the desired amount of background. I like the effect achieved here of three-dimensional illusion.

18 Countless lava rock spires and stacks tower above sand and surf at Bandon on the southern Oregon Coast. I probably have as many photos of these picturesque spires as this beautiful beach has rocks. Each season, each change of tide, creates new and different images for me to work with. This photo was taken in the early eighties.

19 When I first visited Cape Kiwanda in 1929, I had to hike over a mile to reach it, but for many years now it has been possible to park close to the cape and climb the sand dunes. Unfortunately, the picturesque areas are extremely hazardous, and lives have been lost to the surf.

Since that first visit to Kiwanda, I've revisited the area countless times and photographed the surf and cliffs under every imaginable condition. More than half those visits resulted in no photographs at all. In fact, I often do not even remove my camera from my rucksack. On other occasions, however, I succumb to the temptation of the surf and shoot scores of photographs. Many of those photos have found their way into publications, but far more have found their way into my wastepaper basket.

I have wished I had made greater use of the 35mm camera with all its innovations rather than using bulky, large-format cameras. But at the time, editors preferred to see 4x5s. Still, I count my blessings and am particularly grateful for the increase in film speed. In the old days of the early Kodachrome and Ektachrome, with film speeds of ASA 8 or 10, quality surf action pictures were next to impossible to achieve. This photo was taken in the late seventies.

20 My quest for coastal sunsets usually involves cloud formations reflecting light. This time, in the early eighties, I was on Cannon Beach, Oregon, with my Hasselblad at the end of a beautiful, cloudless day. My 150mm lens viewed the composition as I liked it and this image was the result. I recall setting the shutter speed at 250th of a second to catch the offshore maneuvers of the gulls.

21 Autumn and winter months are, in my opinion, the best time to visit the Oregon Coast, for it is during those months that surf and atmospheric conditions are apt to be the most spectacular.

Early January 1988 found me out on the point of Ecola State Park as a new day was born. Minute by minute, the scene changed as the sun's rays beamed through a veil of fog, illuminating the waves bound for Crescent Beach.

22 In 1947, my friend, Wally Eagle, joined me for a day of fishing the Gallatin River, a few miles north of his home in West Yellowstone, Montana. The Gallatin is a familiar rendezvous for natives of the area, and Wally apparently knows the favorite playground of every trout in the stream. Taken on 4x5 Kodachrome, which was still available at the time, this photo has retained its original color.

23 Ice caves have been my nemesis on a couple of different occasions. One summer day in the early seventies, Mira and I, along with the Lindhjem family, visited Mt. Rainier's ice caves. The caves were magnificent. We explored several rooms and tunnels underneath Paradise Glacier and took quite a few pictures, but did not get all we wanted.

A few days later, in midweek, Mira and I again hiked up the trail. The weather was terrific, and I rushed on up the trail as fast as I could. Just as I arrived at the entrance of the cave, I met a young photographer coming out, and as we paused to exchange greetings, hundreds of tons of ice collapsed, barely missing us. Luckily for me, I had paused to say hello.

24 In the early fifties, I was traveling on an unfamiliar, rural dirt road in eastern Oregon between Kimberly and Mitchell when I noticed a couple of deer feeding near the road. I braked and climbed out as fast as I could, hoping to get a shot of the deer with a rather interesting background setting.

Of course, they took off, but my closer observation of the picturesque scene—the gently curving rows of the grainfield leading to the weathered barn and autumn-tinted poplar trees—showed me that I had a picture, one I would never see quite this way again.

25 One foggy, drizzly morning in early August in the seventies, I was scouting potential foreground interests for compositions. I wanted to feature either Mt. Rainier or the Tatoosh Range, but I was impressed by this lonesome Indian paintbrush surrounded by a carpet of blue lupine. Lighting was ideal for maximum detail and color rendition.

26 Please see copy on page facing Plate 26.

27 I believe it was in the late forties that I saw a spectacular photo of the shoreline of Hawaii. Although I had not noted the location, the picture impressed me so vividly I immediately recognized the setting when I first viewed the Na Pali Coast on

Kauai Island in Hawaii, while covering an assignment for United Airlines in 1952.

Mira and I were on the scene again in the early sixties, when this particular photo was captured. After taking a few pictures some distance from the cliffs, we edged our way along a rocky shoreline as far as we dared go. Then I climbed atop a four-foot-high, offshore rock with surf lapping around my feet. I was sorely tempted to leap for safety, but the most explosive surf action was occurring within easy reach of my 250mm Hasselblad lens, and we held our ground, taking pictures until sunset.

28 For me, the highlight of 1952 was my assignment in Hawaii. I had just about come to the conclusion that assignments were not my cup of tea when this one came my way. By April I was riding the waves in the prow of an outrigger canoe, facing seaward and photographing another outrigger and surfers riding the same wave.

It was a thrilling and productive experience. There was no problem with the 35mm Nikon, except in trying to keep it dry. This shot was taken with 35mm Kodachrome.

29 The rays of the setting sun illuminate the Na Pali coastline, where the mountains rise four thousand feet above the sea. My Hasselblad did a good day's work, climaxed by this 250mm image, and I feel privileged to pass along some of the beauty of that experience. This photo dates from the sixties.

30 In the fifties, I revisited a historic region which had recently been opened up for general travel by a new route between Montana and Idaho known as the Lola Pass Highway. It was autumn, and I camped on the Lochsa River. When I awoke, the area was covered with frost, and I saw the rising sun penetrate through the depths of the canyon.

As usual, I started getting my 4x5 camera set up on the tripod and put my meter into action. I wish I had grabbed my 35mm Nikon with its built-in meter and instant focusing. Instead, I managed only two 4x5 exposures and one 35mm before the sun melted the frost.

31 I took this 4x5 photo in the sixties. It captures a small part of the beauty of an area aptly called Cathedral In The Desert. This and other striking

photographic opportunities were made possible when Ben and Harriet Andrews and I chartered a light plane for a flight to the upper end of Lake Powell. Ben and Harriet were both prominent camera clubbers and as interested in photographing as I, so we chartered a small boat and guide for a day exploring the tributary canyons of Lake Powell. It was a day I will never forget.

As most folks know, Lake Powell was created by the construction of the extremely controversial Glen Canyon Dam on the Colorado River. The lake is nearly two hundred miles long and, combined with its countless tributaries and canyons, creates a total of almost two thousand miles of shoreline.

32 In late September of 1984, my present wife, Doris, and I spent a couple of weeks in Wyoming plagued by snow, rain, and clouds. In other words, "nonphotographic" weather for the photos we had planned to take in Yellowstone and Grand Teton national parks.

One cold, wet evening, we arrived at Colter Bay on Jackson Lake. Next morning, I came out of hibernation and was astounded to witness the unveiling of Mt. Moran. I grabbed both cameras and went into action for an exciting fifteen minutes as Mt. Moran, sporting a new robe of autumn snow, played hide and seek. Then the Tetons disappeared again for the remainder of our few days' stay in the area.

33 Fellow photographer Russ Lamb and I paid an autumn visit to Yellowstone and Teton national parks in the midseventies. While exploring the Jackson Hole region, we discovered this colorful setting in Teton National Forest, to the east of the national park. Our patience and persistence were rewarded when sunlight found an opening in the clouds and partially illuminated the landscape.

34 On a beautiful, autumn day in the late forties, Mira, Eleanor, and I visited Devil's Tower National Monument. Autumn color along the approach to the tower did its best to steal the show, and a village of prairie dogs delayed our arrival by enthusiastically entering into our photographic activities.

35 In 1947, I photographed this little pine tree clinging tenaciously and stubbornly to the top of a picturesquely sculptured sandstone formation in

Zion National Park. Forty years later, when I took this photo, the tree seemed to be no bigger. Apparently its roots have a difficult time finding sufficient food and moisture, and the prevailing winds have sculptured it into a natural bonsai.

36 Once in the late fifties, Mira and I flew with all our camera equipment to El Paso, Texas, en route to an ambitious photo coverage of springtime gardens, antebellum houses, and points of interest in the South. We then hired a car and drove to Carlsbad Caverns National Park, New Mexico.

Due to time and other limitations, I chose to use only my 35mm Nikon and was able to take several photos of a variety of formations, including this one of the Big Room, with time exposures for the artificial lighting in the cavern supplemented by flashbulbs in my own reflectors.

37 Please see copy on page facing Plate 37.

38 Alpine flower meadows around the timberline base of Mt. Rainier are unsurpassed anywhere in the world, and many are within easy reach of visitors. One day in the seventies, a hike to Mazama Ridge, just east of Paradise Valley, unveiled countless visual opportunities for hikers and camera buffs.

39 Northhead Lighthouse, at the mouth of the Columbia, continues to lure me back. I am always hoping surf and weather will satisfy my constant search for perfection. Though that will never occur, much enjoyment and many photos have resulted.

Surprisingly, it wasn't until June of 1988 that I saw the potential of this tree-framed vista. Thankfully, such opportunities continue to present themselves for discovery. Observation is the key.

40 On a clear, winter day in 1982, I chartered a small plane to circle Mt. St. Helens. With my Hasselblad I photographed the mountain from various angles and circled it several times at several elevations. All the time, I tried to identify landmarks which had once been familiar to me. Before 1980, those treeless slopes had been beautiful parklands and forest surrounding Spirit Lake.

41 I consider Mt. Shuksan, Washington, the most photogenic mountain in America. The mountain

itself is situated in the North Cascades National Park and has been the target of my camera more times than I can count.

However, until October 1985 when this picture was taken, I had not obtained a really good photo of the mountain with the sunset glow illuminating its glaciers and crags. Often, the sun drops down behind Mt. Baker, which is west of Mt. Shuksan, and the sunset rays never reach Shuksan at all.

42 It's not hard to understand why Washington's Glenwood Valley lures countless camera enthusiasts every October and is a must on the schedule for various Northwest camera clubs. My 4x5 Linhoff turned out this image in the seventies, when the lofty cone of Mt. Adams had donned an early season robe of ermine.

43 This spectacular cleft in the lava walls of the Columbia Gorge National Scenic Area is directly beside the highway on the Oregon side of the Columbia River. I set up my 4x5 camera on the tripod one autumn morning in the early sixties and adjusted a delayed-action shutter so I could dash over to that nearby log.

It is during these autumn days that the dramatic backlighting I prefer occurs. Water levels are lower too, and it's easier to hike to the hundred-foot waterfall at the end of Oneonta Gorge.

44 Early morning mists were melting away in sunlight, and I was enjoying the beauty and solitude of Redwood National Park near Crescent City, California, one day in the sixties. The ethereal atmosphere was near ideal, and the haze created effects that cannot be captured under other conditions.

45 Sugarcane tassels glinting in Hawaiian sunlight appealed to my photographic eye when I first visited the Islands in 1952. Finally in 1972, on the island of Kauai, I chose a ground level viewpoint and trained the Nikon on this grouping against a mountain range enveloped in shadow.

46 One of my favorite autumn haunts is a walk along the banks of this small stream in the southern Washington Cascades, near the base of Mt. Adams. It's a bit more difficult to notice the intimate details of nature in a region where scenic grandeur

abounds, but the tranquility and beauty of this rippling water in the seventies was its own reward.

47 Another prime example of what can be discovered and photographed when all is not well with the primary subject occurred during a cloudy autumn day in 1985 in Washington's Cascade Range. Had the snow-clad mountains been clear, it's unlikely I would have noticed the mountain ash clustered around the hemlock snag. This is a lesson I've learned countless times: there is usually something good beneath every cloud.

48 Please see copy on page facing Plate 48.

49 An abundance of golden wildflowers carpeted the Painted Hills in central Oregon when Doris and I visited the area in late May 1979. Each spring since, I return in the hope that the unforgettable experience will repeat, but the flowers have never reappeared so dramatically.

Some botanists theorize that a tremendous cloudburst, which followed my 1979 visit, washed the fragile soil off the hills and into the flats, burying the flower seeds so deep that they could not grow.

50 It was a clear, hot day in the early sixties, in the Skyrocket Hills of southeastern Washington, when I took this wheat harvest scene. It was an exciting day of photography because the hills created lighting situations that were favorable from dawn until dusk, and I got carried away both physically and mentally. I chased combines up and down the hills, giving little thought to the fact that the temperature was between 105 and 110 degrees in the shade. The result was a number of really exciting pictures and a case of dehydration that laid me low for several days.

51 There are two ways to photograph the entire bowl of Crater Lake: with a circuit camera, or from the air above the lake. My first air views were taken from the eighteen thousand-foot altitude because I use a standard focal length lens on my 4x5 camera. This time, after a turbulent flight through clouds in July of 1980, I chose to use a wide angle and captured outstanding shots from fourteen thousand feet.

52 I was fortunate to be at timberline in the Cascade Range one day in the late forties when

sunset's alpenglow painted the landscape in rosy hues. This photo is one that revives wonderful memories and, hopefully, shares them with others.

53 I had first learned of the Rainbow Bridge during my youth, when I read Zane Grey's enthralling novel, *The Rainbow Trail*. His vivid descriptions and his story were indelibly impressed on my mind. Now here I was, in 1947, actually exploring the wonders of those fantastically beautiful canyons. Of course, that was years before the Rainbow Bridge was made easily accessible via boat on Lake Powell.

After miles of traveling—some by hiking and some on the back of a mule—in the intense, desert heat, we reached the fabulous Rainbow Bridge in the evening and camped in a nearby cliffside cave. The solitude was broken only by the lazy stomping of the pack animals and a noisy chorus of frogs vibrating beside a pool. Next day, a beautiful hike down the canyon to the Colorado River, skinny dipping in a clear, warm pool beneath the bridge, and a bagful of 4x5 Ektachrome images were generous rewards for our efforts.

54 Late afternoon sunlight blazed across the sand dunes of Monument Valley on the Arizona-Utah boundary, as a Navajo couple rode obligingly across the scene with their colt. The photo, taken during one of my earliest visits, in the forties, was made possible with the assistance of Harry Goulding, the Navajo Indian trader.

55 Pleasant Valley, Colorado, has greeted me with entirely different moods of weather and color. Undoubtedly, the region is not always so considerate, but I have only pleasant and exciting memories and a wealth of colorful photos. This photo was taken one autumn in the early seventies.

56 Doris and I visited Yellowstone National Park in mid-June 1983. We planned to take advantage of water volume at Yellowstone Falls, favorable lighting inside the canyon, and early-morning illumination of the falls. The rainbow rising in the mist below my camera position was a plus.

57 Action ski shots are usually planned. This photo was taken on the slopes of Squaw Valley, California, in the late fifties on old, slow-speed

Ektachrome film. Internationally-known ski racer, Yves Latreille, along with Miss Pat Riley and Miss Johnny Rankin were skiing for my camera on that beautiful February day.

I had already studied the terrain and the lighting on previous runs and skied down in front of the other three, being careful not to track slopes that I intended to use in my pictures.

58 During our 1941 Canadian Rockies adventure, Walt Dyke and I decided to hike into the Tonquin Valley from Mt. Edith Cavell. Studying our map, we saw that the designated trail was not the shortest, so we took a more direct approach. A couple of hours later, we were helplessly struggling across a huge rock slide, which had boulders as large as houses.

It was growing dark before we finally reached our destination and hurriedly pitched camp. Next morning, we opened the tent flap and were enthusiastically greeted by swarms of mosquitoes and a panoramic view of the magnificent Rampart Range towering above Amethyst Lake.

59–60 It was an afternoon in 1987 when Scott Krueter and I hiked up the slickrock (sandstone) slopes of Arches National Park toward Delicate Arch. My first visit to this region was in 1926 when I drove my 1921 Ford across the desert between Grand Junction, Colorado, and Price, Utah, on a 120-degree day in August and had twelve flat tires as the cold patches on my inner tubes melted.

Then, in the summer of 1947, Mira, Eleanor, and I hiked up these same slopes. In spite of the heat, we explored the area for vantage points from which to photograph the arch. Now, in 1987, no time need be wasted as Scott and I arrived to find the desired lighting and turned our cameras loose.

61 It was in 1950 that I hiked up the trail to the Little Beehive, a few miles above Lake Louise, and photographed one of the most spectacular views I have ever seen. The trail climbs in gentle grades for miles through forests to Lake Agnes, then on up another mile of open terrain to this vantage point, where the grandeur of the Canadian Rockies is unfurled.

62 A major autumn snowstorm in the sixties cut short my plans for two weeks of photography in Wyoming and Montana by closing the highway between Cook City and Red Lodge, so I drove through the blizzard to Glacier National Park. The fury of the storm abated, but that night, as I lay awake planning the great day of shooting ahead, a strong wind came up and by daylight all the autumn foliage was gone. Completely frustrated, I drove back to Portland with only a few 4x5 and 35mm color photos, such as this one of St. Mary's Lake, to show for my autumn adventure.

63 In 1977, Doris and I were enjoying our honeymoon in Hawaii when I was impressed by the rhythm of Pacific surf washing the coral sand beach of Kaanapali on Maui Island. My Leica went into action and several striking color slides resulted.

64 One beautiful spring day in the Santa Ynez Valley in the early seventies, I climbed a wire fence and hiked through pastureland to compose this picture of a cluster of poppie blossoms with oak trees silhouetted against a blue sky. To me, this image best captures the beauty of California's rural countryside, which is so rapidly disappearing under the onslaught of urban and industrial development.

65 An easy mile hike from the McKenzie Pass Highway takes you to two waterfalls just inside the Three Sisters Wilderness in Oregon's Cascade Mountains. Lower Proxy, pictured here in the seventies, initially reveals itself from a trail's-end vantage point and resembles several waterfalls I've seen. But a scramble down a steep, log-obstructed slope and across a swampy area opens up an entirely different world of beauty drenched in spray. Here is one of my favorite outdoor photo studios.

66 Wildflowers are temperamental, but few are more undependable than bear grass, also known as Indian basket grass. In the Mt. Hood area, bear grass may stage a dramatic and abundant show as it did one year in the sixties, and another year there will not be a single blossom on a hundred plants.

67 I am sure that many photographers traveling the U.S. Forest Service road between Trout Lake and Randall, Washington, have been charmed into exposing film as they paused beside this cascading stream, pictured here in 1986.

I first photographed the waterfall many years ago when the road was only a rough and muddy access to Takhlakh Lake and timber west of Mt. Adams, and I spent a couple of hours cleaning away a mess of brush and small logs. I've photographed it several times since, and each time varying water and light created a different beauty.

68 Each summer a tiny lake is reborn on the slopes of Park Ridge in the Mt. Jefferson Wilderness area in Oregon's Cascade Range. It was a heavy snow year in the forties when Dwight Watson and I hiked into Jefferson Park, heart of the Wilderness, and found the lake just putting in its appearance in August.

69 It was just after sunrise, on a crisp autumn morning in the eighties, and I was driving up the Long Beach Peninsula from Ilwaco, Washington. Intrigued by the play of sunlight through fog-veiled trees on the far shore of a small lake and anticipating some action, I grabbed my Linhoff.

I have driven by this little lake numerous times without so much as a second glance. It just isn't a photogenic subject under normal circumstances, but on that particular day, I was at the right place.

70 Numerous trails in the Columbia River Gorge Scenic Area lure hikers year-round, and the Eagle Creek Trail is perhaps the most popular of all. In October in the midsixties, veiled sunlight created ideal conditions on the forest floor. I adjusted my shutter for a delayed-action exposure that caught me on the trail under old-growth Douglas fir.

71 Please see copy on page facing Plate 71.

72 One autumn day in the early sixties, I was exploring back roads and hinterlands of southern Utah. The daylight hours were coming to an end when I noticed the reflection of sandstone cliffs illuminating the shallow waters of the Escalante River. The light was fading fast, so I took a hurried meter reading before exposing a couple of 4x5s.

73 In the fifties, I was hiking back down Oregon's Eagle Creek Trail alone when I met an excited group of hikers on a narrow ledge. They called my attention to the solar phenomenon created when the sun's rays illuminate frost crystals at a very high altitude.

74 From the standpoint of soil and climate, several Pacific Northwest valleys have proven ideal for raising a variety of flowering bulbs. Each spring, vast fields of commercially-grown daffodils and tulips burst into bloom in the Skagit, Puyallup, and Lewis river valleys. It was April 1988 when I photographed the colorful glory of this Willamette Valley field of tulips on the Wooden Shoe Bulb Farm.

75 My contention that lighting is important in making an attractive landscape picture is successfully disputed here. This old oak tree surrounded by wildflowers above the Klickitat River Canyon in southern Washington proved a rewarding subject for my Linhoff one day in the eighties, despite an angle of sunlight I would normally consider unfavorable.

76 One summer night in the early seventies, a freak electrical storm thundered northward from its origin in the Cascade Range, crossed Portland, Oregon, and continued on into Washington. I say "freak storm" because electrical storms are rare in western Oregon, and I have never seen one equal to this one in intensity. I enjoyed the spectacle from a grand viewpoint near my home, recording multiple flashes with an exposure of less than three minutes.

77 Occasionally, the east wind blows across the Cascade and Coast ranges out to the Pacific. When this occurs in winter and the surf is up, it creates opportunities for striking pictures as banners of spindrift sail off foam-crested breakers racing shoreward. This view was taken in the late seventies from the shoulder of Neahkahnie Mountain.

78 Few Oregonians, including myself, fully appreciated the dunes running forty or fifty miles along the central Oregon Coast. Then in the sixties, Senator Richard Neuberger and others helped to establish the dunes as a National Recreation Area.

Photographing the dunes in the seventies, I found they sheltered islands of vegetation, and provided a constantly changing palette tempered by the hazards of wind-blown sand.

79 Each time I visit Olympic Rain Forest in Olympic National Park, several previously unnoticed images find their way into the lenses of my cameras. One October day, in the early seventies,

autumn-tinted vine maple leaves on the mossy floor of Quinault Valley forest caught my eye.

80 Fog is the rule, not the exception, on Cape Lookout Trail on the Oregon Coast and it usually enhances the photographic image. Even during the summer, high fog hovers at almost the same altitude as the forested crest of the cape. This day in the early eighties was no exception.

81 Bright sunlight creates contrasting highlights and shadows that are extremely difficult for color film to handle satisfactorily. Luckily, it was an overcast day in October in the seventies, in the foothills of Washington's Cascade Range, when I took this shot of club moss and sword fern.

82 The beach at Bandon, on the southern Oregon Coast, is one of the most beautiful beaches in the world. And each year, as this photo from the late seventies testifies, flowering gorse along the shoreline enhances Bandon's beauty in early spring.

83 Compared to other famed Oregon Coast spectacles like Cape Kiwanda, Shore Acres came under fire from my cameras rather late in my career. I had done some intimate images of sculptured sandstone, but the spectacular surf action, captured here, had eluded me until the seventies.

84 Please see copy on page facing Plate 84.

85 The sunset hours are an ideal time to turn your camera loose at almost any point along the south rim of the Grand Canyon. It was in the fifties that I found this old monument to the past clinging tenaciously to its wind-swept vantage point.

86 It's difficult to find an exciting subject I haven't previously photographed at Bryce Canyon National Park. On a gorgeous day in May 1987, I hiked down into the great amphitheater twice—no minor deal at my age—with my 4x5 Linhoff, lenses, and tripod and photographed this "exclusive" image. Later, while going through some of my fifty-year-old slides, I discovered a near duplicate Kodachrome composition of the fallen tree. If the setting caught my eye fifty years ago and again in 1987, it is certain other photographers have been attracted to it.

87 & 88 Long famed for its scenic beauty, the Monterey Peninsula has suffered both natural and man-made casualties. Many of the picturesque old cypress trees that lured travelers to this beautiful shoreline have been ravaged by Pacific storms. Others have been destroyed by development.

The famed tree on Cypress Point has suffered years of buffeting by weather and unthinking abuse from visitors. I was shocked to see during my last visit in 1988 that, despite increased protection, the venerable old cypress is no longer as attractive as it was when I photographed it bathed in sunset color during a visit in the late forties.

89 The mouth of Ecola Creek on Cannon Beach is a rendezvous for thousands of seagulls. Bird traffic is particularly heavy in the autumn when a new crop of birds, hatched in the spring on nearby Bird Rocks and Haystack Rock, arrive. My Hasselblad camera went into action just before sunset one day in 1988.

90 This was one of those unplanned shots that took precedence over a previously planned photo session on the Oregon Coast. One day in the mid-eighties, I was looking for a sunset as a stage prop for one of my favorite surf and offshore rock settings, when the surf below the Crescent Beach Trail caught and held my interest.

91 One stormy, November day in the late seventies, Doris and I returned to Shore Acres and found breakers so tremendous and wind-driven spray so saturating that I made only a couple of frustrated attempts to catch a shot. Reluctantly, I gave up and we took time out for lunch. Afternoon found us back again, and as the storm subsided and occasional breaks in the clouds favored us with spots of sunlight, both my cameras went into action.

92 Owens Valley, California, is a region of the West where camera club members gather annually. Here, in November 1965, along the eastern escarpment of the Sierra Nevada, cottonwood, willows, and flowering rabbitbrush create an outdoor workshop for my 4x5 camera.

93 Millions of waterfowl gather at the Tule Lake National Wildlife Refuge in California during their annual migration from Canada to their wintering

home in California's central valleys. In November, in the sixties, a few of them took flight for my camera as sunset silhouetted Mt. Shasta's distant, 14,161-foot volcanic cone.

94 One of my favorite areas in the West is a foot-hill ridge in the Cascade Range, just east of Hood River Valley in northern Oregon and south of the Columbia River. It commands views of Mt. Hood to the south, Mt. Adams to the north, the valley itself, and Mt. Defiance to the west.

This day in April, in the early eighties, was superb for photography. A few days before, my friend, Scott Krueter, and I had experienced very frustrating conditions, when haze almost obscured the mountain. We were at a loss to understand why the haze existed until we arrived home and heard that Mt. St. Helens had staged a minor eruption.

95 It was just forty years after my first visit to Yellowstone National Park that I took this photo of the geyser, Old Faithful. That first visit to the park in late September 1933, I learned that thermal activity and frigid temperatures in the autumn created a great deal more steam. A moment after this photo was taken, the steam from the eruption rose completely out of the photographic composition. It was fortunate that I captured the action when I did.

96 To me, this photo of Joshua trees and granite rocks etched against a vivid sunset captures the unique beauty of Joshua Tree National Monument, overlooking the great Mojave Desert in southern California. I captured this image in May 1982.

97 Please see copy on page facing Plate 97.

98 I've often found that it pays to be constantly on the lookout for unexpected photo opportunities. This time, in October 1985, the surrounding mountains were locked in with clouds, but the timberline meadows of Washington's North Cascades were ablaze with mountain ash and huckleberry.

99 Checkerboard Mesa may be the most stunning of countless sandstone mountains that greet visitors entering Zion National Park, Utah, via the scenic Mt. Carmel Highway from the east. It is a tremendous mountain, sculptured by the elements into thousands of symmetrical squares and rectangles. Once you've made the dozens of decisions a photographer typically makes, all you have to do is choose a viewpoint. This shot was taken in the seventies.

100 Going to a site well-equipped can mean the difference between getting a shot and losing it. Lehman Caves, in eastern Nevada, were illuminated to a minor extent for visitors, but when I entered them in 1947, I was armed with flashbulbs and reflectors to supplement the existing lighting.

101 This is one of very few Ektachrome transparencies from the late forties that has not faded beyond recovery. One beautiful day in January, Virginia Nelson and I stood on the summit of Hoodoo Butte in Oregon's Central Cascade Range. Since then, fire has destroyed the forest around this popular ski area and the beauty we saw has vanished.

102 Washington and Oregon must concede to the Rocky Mountain states when it comes to the annual show of golden aspen foliage. But this grove on an Okanogan hillside on the eastern slopes of the Cascade Range caught my eye while I was photographing a cattle drive in the fifties.

103 En route home with models after an extensive trip which included Glacier National Park, Yellowstone, the Tetons, Utah's redrock wonderlands, Death Valley, and Yosemite, I visited Lassen Volcano National Park, California. It was a visit of only a few hours in October 1946, but a really great few hours they turned out to be.

104 The Golden Gate International Exposition on Treasure Island, California, in 1939 provided a memorable experience for Mira, our four-year-old daughter, Eleanor, and me. The visual impact of the unique architecture and landscaping was especially beautiful, illuminated at night by colorful lighting, and I captured many rewarding time-exposure images with my Bantam Special and Kodachrome film.

105 Although I prefer natural landscapes, Seattle Center's Fountain and Space Needle present interesting photo opportunites. Visitors admiring the fountain complicated the time exposure, which occurred for several seconds at dusk in the seventies.

106 It was a day when everything was right, and I happened to be in the right place at the right time. In late July, in the early seventies, Paradise Valley in Mt. Rainier National Park was blooming with lupine and Indian paintbrush, and my 4x5 Linhoff, 135mm lens, and professional Ektachrome film were ready.

107 Wildlife photography is not my number one pursuit. I haven't the patience, nor do I have the necessary persistence. Luckily, neither of those qualities was essential when I recorded this image, taken in the sixties on Hurricane Ridge in Olympic National Park with my Hasselblad. Here the deer virtually ask visitors to take their picture.

108 In February 1976, I enjoyed a great day of skiing on the slopes of Anthony Lakes Ski Resort in Oregon's Elkhorn Range. I would have been taking pictures, but snow fell all day.

Next day, I again drove up from overnight lodging in Baker and the sun was shining. The fantastic beauty of the hour was enhanced by a feeling of solitude and grandeur that can only be experienced when a whole mountain world surrounds a single person. It's an experience impossible to record, but this photo brings back the memory for me.

109 Coated with ice from snow that had melted and frozen, the switch-back trail up the steep slope of Sauk Mountain was almost impossible to navigate in ordinary hiking boots when I hiked it in October 1977. I noticed this cluster of windblown evergreens as I clambered up to the summit.

110 Please see copy on page facing Plate 110.

111 Seldom are the redwoods more entrancing than when enveloped in the low-hanging fog I experienced during this visit to northern California in the sixties. The harsh contrasts of bright sunlight and dark shadow cannot be fully assimilated by either the human eye or the camera lens. Appreciate your blessings if you happen to be in the magnificent force of a day like this.

112 Sometimes I'm lucky. On an autumn day in the early sixties, while exploring southern Utah backcountry, I came across this setting at sunset. The roads in the area were rural and access to this

particular spot was nothing but sand and gravel with a few tracks in it. It wasn't a destination, it was just a spot I happened to run across in my exploring.

I was told the formations I had photographed were in an area called "Kodachrome Flats," now called Kodachrome Basin State Park. The name was a clue that other photographers had preceded me.

113 My introduction to Pleasant Valley in southwestern Colorado was this peaceful scene, and I became so enamored with the area that I have returned several times since. This photo, taken in the early sixties, shows the Mt. Sneffels Range of the San Juan Mountains.

114 This setting, at the foot of Mt. Shuksan in Washington's Mt. Baker National Forest, is often overlooked. I'm glad I did notice and capitalize on it that day in the early seventies. Since then, I have visited the little lake several times, but neither the blue boat nor the autumn colors favored me again.

115 In the late seventies, I made plans with Bob Griffith and Russ Lamb to hike into Idaho's Sawtooth Wilderness area. We hired a packer to transport our camping gear and food, and Russ and I took our Linhoff and Hasselblad cameras, heavy tripods, and extra film magazines.

At Lake Alice there was a steep trail, and Bob Griffith began suffering severely from a flu-type cold. A light snowfall greeted our arrival at camp, and that night and the following day were miserable for Bob. Fortunately, clear weather eventually prevailed, Bob got better, and we hiked back down the trail where I took this photo of El Capitan.

116 One spring day in the sixties, Mira and I were hoping for a beautiful sunset across the Pacific surf, where it plays along the rock-studded shoreline of the Monterey Peninsula, when we noticed some deer feeding among cypress trees atop a ridge.

Accustomed to human intrusion, the deer cooperated by paying no attention to us as I set up my tripod and 4x5 camera. Even the sunset cooperated for a brief blaze of glory.

117 I hoped for a little autumn color when I left the motel in Ilwaco at daybreak, and I couldn't have been more pleased with pictorial conditions. I took this photo in the late sixties, but it was not the first time this covered bridge, now a historic landmark, attracted the eye of my camera. Nor was it the last.

118 We were in Washington's North Cascades, and it seemed the only sensible thing we could do was leave and return when weather conditions were more favorable. Instead, we climbed up into those frustrating clouds that obscure mountain peaks and discovered a new world of beauty awaiting our cameras. Our experience on that autumn day in 1986 re-emphasized the importance of persistence and observation in the art of photography.

119 One early autumn morning in the sixties, Mira and I were headed for Tillamook Bay with high hopes we could shoot some unusual pictures of salmon fishermen on fog-veiled waters. When these three evergreen trees standing alone in a pasture caught our eye, I immediately parked the car and grabbed the camera. Experience has taught me that some of the most pleasing renditions pictorially are achieved by shooting against the light.

Just as our cameras went into action, the rising sun came over the mountains in the distance and cast its colorful beams through the fog surrounding the trees. This thrilling beginning for a new day gave us the backlighting we prefer.

120 One autumn morning in the early eighties, a thin veil of fog created the ethereal, atmospheric effect that I love. Crescent Beach in Oregon was the place, and my Hasselblad was the camera.

The early morning sun burst over the tree-ringed hills of Ecola State Park, illuminating the lazy waves as they washed the rock-studded sands of the beach. Waves and mist created images of elusive beauty that I tried to capture on film before the fog melted away.

121 As the earth turns and moves in space, so the sun's position lends itself to favored compositions of offshore rocks, sand, clouds, and reflecting surf. Even the tides and surf turbulence affect the image. The Needles at Cannon Beach, Oregon, posed for this photo in November 1985. Sun, surf, and sky were all in a cooperative mood.

122 On this autumn day in the sixties, during a solo hike to the Eagle Creek Punch Bowl, I dispensed with encumbering clothes and, with my 4x5 camera and tripod held high, swam and waded to a point of land just below the falls to take this shot. I especially like the lighting and the touch of autumn haze that helped to make this photo just a bit different from others I've taken here.

123 Picture Lake, shown in the foreground of this photo, nearby Highwood Lake, and Heather Meadows are popular meeting places for photographers and sightseers, especially during the autumn months when the huckleberry and mountain ash are unbelievably colorful. But the very fact that Mt. Shuksan and the lakes in Heather Meadows are so photogenic and so thoroughly photographed by thousands of photographers presents a tremendous challenge to anyone who photographs there.

The atmosphere on this early October morning in the mideighties achieved the near impossible. It created a photographic image of unique beauty.

124 One of my ambitious winter photographic trips through the West in the fifties included visits to the Grand Canyon, Oak Creek and Bryce canyons, Alta Utah Ski Resort, and Sun Valley. With few exceptions, the photographs from that trip were very satisfactory, but after thirty years, most of the 4x5 transparencies have deteriorated in color. Fortunately, this photo of an icicle-festooned wall in Oak Creek Canyon has retained its original color.

125 Never have I seen Bryce Canyon as beautiful as during my winter visit in the fifties. The weather, following a light snowfall on a base of several feet of old snow, was frigid but ideal for photography, and the colors in the amphitheater were superb.

Later, I skied down onto the floor of the canyon. This was an event long remembered for the photos that resulted, but most of all for the difficulty of climbing back to the rim. Exhausted after hours of seemingly hopeless struggle with my skis repeatedly breaking through the thin crust into deep powder, I finally reached the rim at dusk.

126 This old pine failed to reach the venerable age for which bristlecones are famed, but it created its own artistic monument to past glory at the twelve thousand-foot crest of the White Mountains on the California/Nevada state line.

I drove up to this high elevation from the Owens Valley on a road which a heavy, November blanket of snow in the early sixties had made hazardous. A short hike revealed this setting. I like the color and design, despite the direct, flat angle of the light.

127 In 1987, after a glorious day of photography at Dead Horse Point overlooking the Canyonlands National Park and a fruitful hike around Delicate Arch, Scott Krueter and I were returning to Moab for some much-needed rest. Suddenly, we saw the beauty of the last rays of sunlight painting the landscape of the Courthouse Towers. We were so enthralled we ignored our cameras until it was almost too late to capture the fleeting experience on film.

128 Cape Kiwanda and the Pacific surf never stage the same show twice. I keep going back hoping to get in on a blockbuster. I usually pack two cameras and lots of film. Sometimes I return with no good pictures, and often my cameras suffer from salt spray, which is deadly for delicate mechanisms and for critical shutters and lenses. On rare occasions I'm lucky enough to get a winning photo.

This one was snapped during a brief period of sunlight on an uncomfortably cold day in the sixties. Eastman Kodak appreciated my patience and good fortune and displayed the image as a 12 x 60-foot Colorama in Grand Central Station, New York.

129 After a day of skiing on Mt. Hood in the fifties, I stopped for a visit with my friend, Hal Lidell, at Government Camp. His cabin was all decked out in a new robe of snow, and I enlisted his help to take this Christmas card scene with my 4x5 Speed Graphic on a tripod for a time exposure.

130 Around Christmas of 1978, Doris and I were on the Larch Mountain Road, hoping it might be open to the summit, when fresh snow and bright sunlight lured me out of the car with my Linhoff 4x5. The snow was much deeper than expected and I waded in, locating several settings that I liked. For this shot I used a lens that would capture a clear image of the sun without refraction.

131 Each time I revisit Rainbow Bridge via boat on Lake Powell from Glen Canyon Dam on the Colorado River, memories return of my first visit

via the Rainbow Trail from Navajo Lodge, Arizona. Needless to say, these recent visits cannot produce equally impressive feelings.

The miles of hiking through canyon labyrinths, the massive grandeur of the land, and the solitude of my first visit can be relived only in memory. When this photo was taken in the mideighties, these towering canyon walls echoed the lively chatter of people and the hum and roar of motorboats.

132 Under normal lighting conditions, Grand Canyon is a frustrating photo subject. But one June afternoon in the late fifties, I was favored by a fast-moving series of thunderstorms. The landscape seemed to change by the minute as clouds and sunlight chased each other across the canyon.

133 A winter day in 1947, following a few days of winter photography in northern Washington, I decided to put up for the night at a motel near Kelso and head to Spirit Lake before dawn. When I reached the lake, I found it free of ice and snow. At first this was a disappointment. I had planned to ski across to the north shore, where views of Mt. St. Helens awaited my camera, and the open lake dictated a much longer and more difficult route.

But a few inches of new snow on a good base of old made for easy going, and when I reached the first viewpoint at Harmony Falls, I realized my good fortune. The calm morning atmosphere set the stage for near-perfect reflections of the snow-draped mountain in the ice-free lake. Best of all, 4x5 Kodachrome was still available, and all these photos are as colorful as the day they were exposed.

134 Just a maple leaf, but its coloration was so beautiful, I had to preserve it on film. I was heading for the Oregon Coast via Sunset Highway one late October morning in the sixties when I stopped in a rest area and put my 4x5 camera into action.

135 Washington Forest on the steep shores of Swift Reservoir near Mt. St. Helens, Washington, attracted my camera eye one autumn day in the sixties. I emphasized the sunlight glinting from the wind-rippled lake surface by using a Sparkle Filter.

136 In March 1988, my friend, Scott Krueter, and I were en route to poppie fields on the edge of

the Mojave Desert in southern California. I always plan for multiple photographic opportunities on any extended trip, and this was no exception.

Mt. Shasta was familiar to my camera, as my first visit there, en route to Oregon in 1926, was a lengthy one. I had obtained a job in a box factory in Mt. Shasta City, and on Labor Day Weekend, I climbed to the mountain's fourteen thousand-foot summit. It was my first major mountain ascent, and the experience remains vivid in my memory. During the sixty-odd years since, I have recorded various views of the mountain from virtually every angle.

137 En route home from a visit to Takhlakh Lake in the Pinchot National Forest with my neighbor, Dave Bronson, I was attracted by a kaleidoscope of autumn color in the dense evergreen forest beside the gravel road. Here the road had opened a window to the sunlight, and the normally pastel vine maple was rich with color. Seldom have I enjoyed such a show as was staged that autumn in the sixties.

138 It is difficult to record on film the full beauty of Multnomah Falls from Oregon's Columbia River Highway. The tremendous cliffs over which the stream plunges face directly north and seldom get sufficient light to enhance the view from a photographic standpoint, although at times I have taken advantage of reflected light from a passing cloud.

It was in late October in the early eighties that my assistant, Rick Schafer, and I were at the falls. The autumn coloring was unusually vivid, but we did not have the light we needed. Missing the light, we took advantage of what we did have.

139 One daybreak in December 1987, I took this panoramic view on the north Oregon Coast. Well before sunrise, I had started the mile-and-a-half hike from Indian Beach up the Tillamook Trail, hoping to catch a sunrise over the rugged coast from a vantage point I had used in the fifties.

The sunrise this day escaped my camera because I couldn't find the vantage point in time. During those thirty-odd years, evergreen trees had grown up and screened the view, making it unrecognizable. By the time I located another precarious point for my camera tripod, atmospheric conditions were again favorable and I was able to compose this image of fog-veiled shoreline and coastal mountains.

BIOGRAPHICAL NOTES

1907 Born February 13 on his parents' farm near Grafton, Illinois. Attended one-room school-house until age ten.

1917 Family moves to small town of Jerseyville, Illinois.

1918 Father passes away.

1921 Moves to Kansas City, Missouri, with his mother in order to be closer to relatives.

1922 Receives his first Brownie box camera.

1923 Takes his first impressionistic photograph while working as a janitor. Exposure is due to error and luck. "Union Station at Night with Snow" wins award in *Kansas City Star* and is subsequently published in the *Illustrated London News*.

1924 Spends the summer working in the wheatfields of Kansas and Nebraska. This labor gives Ray the work ethic that stays with him the rest of his life.

1925 Another summer in the wheatfields of Kansas and Nebraska permits him to explore the Front Range area of the Rockies in Colorado.

1926 Transient labor gives him the time to visit Bryce Canyon, en route to Portland, Oregon. Works briefly in Shasta City, California, climbs Mt. Shasta, and arrives in Portland after picking apples in the Hood River Valley, Oregon.

1928 Receives temporary job with Claude Palmer's Photo Art Studio, Portland. Claude is a self-taught perfectionist, who is free with advice. His example and understanding are among the greatest influences in Ray's life.

1929 Marries Mira Crane, the most influential person in Ray's life and career. Mira shares Ray's passion for the beauty of nature and is his companion on his worldwide travels.

Joins the Mazama Club and makes the first of his sixteen ascents of Mt. Hood. Becomes a founding member of the Columbia Hikers Club, later renamed Wy'east Climbers.

1930 Meets and photographs Hjalmer Hvam (a future U.S. Ski Champion). The friendly co-operation of Hjalmer, Olaf Rodegard, and countless other world-class skiers gives Ray national attention as a ski photographer.

Makes the first of three ascents of Mt. Adams, Washington.

1931 Sells mountain-climbing photographs to the *Kansas City Star Rotogravure* for the first time.

Makes the first of four ascents of Mt. St. Helens, Washington.

1932 His photographs appear in the *Los Angeles Times Rotogravure* for the first time.

1933 Travels through Midwest to five major cities to see newspaper editors.

Visits Chicago's World Fair, where one of his photographs is exhibited in the International Salon of Photography.

Visits Yellowstone and learns the value of autumn conditions in that area.

Makes winter ascent of Mt. Hood.

Climbs Mt. Jefferson, Oregon, with a search party to find the body of his best friend, Don Burkhart, who had died on the mountain.

His photographs of the West appear in the *Chicago Daily News Rotogravure* and the *Chicago Tribune Rotogravure*.

1934 His black-and-white portfolio, "When Winter Comes," is published in Portland.

Hastings House Publishing Company, New York, uses Ray's black-and-white photographs extensively in its calendars.

Makes ascent of Mt. Rainier, Washington.

1935 Daughter, Eleanor, is born.

Makes first sales to major film companies: Eastman Kodak, Agfa, Dupont.

His photographs appear in the *Seattle Times Rotogravure* for the first time.

1936 Photographs the National Ski Races at Mt. Rainier, Washington.

His photographs appear for the first time in the *Milwaukee Journal Rotogravure*.

1937 Photographs the Swiss National Ski Team at Mt. Hood, Oregon.

His photographs appear for the first time in the *Houston Chronicle*.

1938 Makes first use of Kodachrome roll film. Trip through Utah, Arizona, and California proves that early Kodachrome needs improvements.

His photographs appear in the *Baltimore Sun Rotogravure*.

1939 Takes his first 4x5 Kodachrome. Photo is of Crown Point, taken from Chanticleer Point in the Columbia River Gorge. H. S. Crocker Printing Company, San Francisco, uses Ray's color photographs in calendars and special portfolios.

His photographs appear in the *San Francisco Chronicle Rotogravure*.

1940 His photographs appear in the *New York Times Rotogravure* for the first time.

1941 Takes first trip into the Canadian Rockies.

Photo Art Studio is designated a defense industry. Ray spends the war years photographing the Kaiser Shipyards, etc.

1945 Photographs a feature story for *National Geographic*.

Makes a successful proposal to the state of Oregon to turn Smith Rock into a state park.

1946 Launches free-lance career full-time.

Receives several *National Geographic* assignments to illustrate stories on the Northwest and British Columbia.

1947 Free-lance business grows.

Swiss Government invites him to photograph Switzerland.

1948 The first of many trips to New York and other eastern cities to establish working relationships with executives in the publishing and advertising industries.

Handles several assignments for the *Saturday Evening Post.*

1949 Receives first assignment from *Holiday Magazine.*

1950 Receives assignments from Ford, Chrysler, General Motors, etc.

1952 Receives assignment from United Airlines to photograph Hawaii.

1954 Publishes black-and-white portfolio in *U.S. Camera Annual.*

1955 Starts a regular camera and travel column for *U.S. Camera Magazine* with Senator Richard Neuberger frequently providing the text.

1956 Receives assignment from Eastman Kodak to photograph Mt. Shuksan, Washington, for their Colorama display in Grand Central Station, New York City. This is the first of four Coloramas created by Ray.

Holds first of three one-man shows in Eastman Kodak's Gallery.

Bushong Litho publishes a color portfolio of his work.

1957 Photographs ski resorts, including Sun Valley, Squaw Valley, and Sugar Bowl. His reputation as a ski and snow photographer grows.

1959 *U.S. Camera Annual* publishes a color portfolio of his work.

1960 *U.S. Camera Annual* publishes his first large-format book, *Ski and Snow.*

1961 Travels extensively through southeastern states with Mira.

1964 Travels to Switzerland and Austria with Mira.

1967 Presents a slide show with commentary to the Professional Photographers of America National Convention with Oregon Governor Tom McCall.

1968 Graphic Arts Center Printing Company, Portland, Oregon, publishes *Oregon,* a collection of his photographs. Charles H. Belding, publisher; Robert Reynolds, designer; Carl Gohs, author.

1969 Graphic Arts Center publishes *Washington.*

Graphic Arts Center publishes *The Cascade Range.*

The International Exposition of Photography in New York exhibits his prints.

1970 Collaborates with David Muench on another Graphic Arts Center book, *California.*

1971 Rand McNally publishes his *Pacific Coast.*

1972 Graphic Arts Center publishes *Oregon Coast.*

Travels to Norway and New Zealand with Mira.

1973 Graphic Arts Center publishes *Washington II.*

Receives Isaac Walton League Award for conservation publications.

1974 Graphic Arts Center publishes *Oregon II.*

Family illness forces a semi-retirement for three years.

1976 Mira passes away.

Deteriorating eyesight forces cataract surgery.

Environmental Graphics becomes client.

1977 Travels to Austria to visit eye specialists who successfully stabilize deteriorating eyesight.

Marries Doris Schafer.

Is named Distinguished Citizen of Oregon in recognition of his artistry and the national and international acclaim his photographs have brought the state.

Receives Honorary Doctorate of Fine Arts from Linfield College, McMinnville, Oregon.

Receives Governor Tom McCall Award for his contributions to Oregon.

Beautiful West Publications publishes *Western Impressions* with an Atkeson text. The book is dedicated to Mira.

Graphic Arts Center publishes *The World of Mira Atkeson,* a tribute to her photography.

1978 Receives Portland Advertising Federation Award for personal commitment to highest standards of excellence in photography.

Takes photo trip to Hawaii with Doris.

1979 Travels to New York, Washington, D.C., and other eastern cities.

1980 Photographs the eruption of Mt. St. Helens, Washington, the most important environmental event in the Pacific Northwest's recent history.

1982 Receives Western Oregon State College's "Distinguished Service Award" for sharing the beauty of the Northwest with the world.

1986 Receives the Oregon Governor's Art Award.

1987 Graphic Arts Center publishes *Oregon III.* Douglas A. Pfeiffer, editor; Robert Reynolds, designer.

Governor Neil Goldschmidt names Ray Photographer Laureate of Oregon.

1989 Graphic Arts Center publishes *Ray Atkeson: Western Images.*